# THE WORLD OF NASCAR

# STOCK CARS GREATEST RACE: The First and the Fastest

TRADITION BOOKS™
EXCELSIOR, MINNESOTA

BY PHIL BARBER

Published by **Tradition Books**™ and distributed to the
school and library market by **The Child's World**®
P.O. Box 326
Chanhassen, MN 55317-0326
800/599-READ
*http://www.childsworld.com*

**Photo Credits**
Cover and title page: AP/Wide World
AP/Wide World: 6 bottom, 17, 19, 20 (2), 21–25, 27, 28
Corbis: 7 top, 8
International Motor Sports Hall of Fame: 11
Sports Gallery: 5, 13 (Joe Robbins); 14 (Al Messerschmidt); 26 (Tom Riles)

Book production by Shoreline Publishing Group, LLC
Art direction and design by The Design Lab

**Library of Congress Cataloging-in-Publication Data**

Barber, Phil.
  Stock car's greatest race : the first and the fastest / by Phil Barber.
      p. cm. — (The world of NASCAR series)
Includes bibliographical references (p.   ) and index.
  ISBN 1-59187-003-8 (lib. bdg. : alk. paper)
  1. Daytona 500 (Automobile race)—Juvenile literature. [1. Daytona 500 (Automobile race)
2. Stock car racing.] I. Title. II. Series.
  GV1033.5.D39 B37 2002
  796.72—dc21                                    2002004642

Copyright © 2003 by Tradition Publishing Company, LLC

STOCK CAR'S GREATEST RACE

# Table of Contents

I N T R O D U C T I O N

# The Biggest Race of All

O n February 22, 1959, Lee Petty nosed past Johnny Beauchamp in a "**photo finish**" to win the first Daytona 500. A crowd of about 41,000 was on hand to witness the historic event. Petty won $19,050 in prize money.

Oh, how times have changed.

The racing action on the track is just as furious now as it was in 1959. Since then, however, the Daytona 500 has grown into one of the world's biggest sporting events. More than 175,000 fans now show up each February at Daytona International Speedway in Florida to watch the 500-mile (805-kilometer) race. Millions more watch the action on television. When Ward Burton won the 2002 Daytona 500, he walked away with $1.3 million. The total **purse** was $11 million.

Daytona Speedway has built a whole series of events—

called Speedweeks—around the 500. The action includes a 24-hour race, the Rolex 24, and competition between Craftsman trucks. The crown jewel of the weekend remains the Daytona 500, the first and biggest race of the NASCAR season.

"As a racer you try to make it just another race," driver Brett Bodine said in 2001. "But when you walk in this garage area and you go to driver introductions—it's the Daytona 500. It's special."

Here is the story of how a little race on the sand became the biggest thing in stock car racing.

A fish-eye lens creates a picture showing Daytona's track and wide infield.

C H A P T E R   O N E

# The Birthplace of Speed

N o one knows for sure when and where the first "horseless carriages" raced in America. But it is known that by 1903, men were speeding in their

More than 200,000 fans crowd into Daytona to watch stock car's greatest race.

jalopies on Daytona Beach. The site is located along the Atlantic Ocean in Florida, about 250 miles (417 kilometers) north of Miami. The beach might sound like a strange place to race cars. Daytona Beach's wide, flat stretches and hard-packed sand, however, made it perfect for racing.

The first driver to stage a timed run on the beach was Ransom E. Olds. This pioneer's name can still be seen in the cars called Oldsmobiles. Olds

Early racers lined up on the beach in roadsters (top).
Barney Oldfield was another early racing star (bottom).

Crack up! This action from a race in the 1940s shows
how rough-and-tumble early Daytona racing was.

drove up and down the beach in a skinny contraption known as the Pirate. He worked hard to reach faster and faster speeds and post quicker and quicker times. People came out to watch these "newfangled" machines do their stuff. Soon Daytona Beach was nicknamed "the Birthplace of Speed."

The time trials moved elsewhere, but people in eastern Florida needed something to satisfy their need for speed. They found the answer in stock cars.

The first stock car course in Daytona Beach was like nothing anybody had raced on before. The course ran about 1.5 miles (2.4 kilometers) north along the beach. It then shot straight into town before heading south again on a paved, public roadway. The two straightaways were connected by **banked** turns on sand. Other than during World War II, the engines revved every year from 1936 to 1958.

One of the men who entered the first race in 1936 was a local mechanic named William H. G. France. He finished fifth. Ten years later, France stopped driving and began to promote stock car racing and motorcycle racing on the beach. In early 1947, he founded NASCAR—the National Association of Stock Car Automobile Racing. France is now honored as a pioneer of racing. The 6 foot 5 inch (196 centimeter) man was known as Big Bill, while his son was Little Bill. Little Bill later became the president of NASCAR after his father. Statues of Big Bill and his wife, Anne, stand outside Daytona International Speedway today.

By the 1950s, Big Bill France saw that beach racing would not last forever. Too many people were moving to sunny Florida. They needed homes and schools and places for recreation. The beach was becoming too popular with visitors to use for racing. In 1953, Big Bill came up with a big idea. He proposed a permanent raceway. Two years later, work began a new $2.9-million facility. Some called it a crazy dream. France and his supporters got the last laugh when Daytona International Speedway opened in 1959.

## MONKEY WRENCH

The beach-racing days of Daytona were full of characters. Captain Malcolm Campbell was a British adventurer and millionaire. He set a land speed record at Daytona in 1931. Lloyd Seay showed up in the late 1930s. Seay would come out of the old North Turn with his left-side wheels in the air. Seay might have been one of the greatest racers ever, but he died at 21. Another driver, Tim Flock, kept a monkey he called Jocko Flocko. The pet accompanied Flock in a few races, perched on his shoulder.

Big Bill France started out as a driver and became the founder of NASCAR.

CHAPTER TWO

# Pavement of Dreams

T here are a lot of reasons that fans love Daytona

International Speedway. Maybe they love the seagulls

gliding around Lake Lloyd, the body of water in the

**infield.** They might gaze at the palm trees along Victory

Lane. Perhaps they like the sound of jet engines from the

airport next door. Mostly, of course, they love the awesome

racing action on the track.

The 2.5-mile (4.1-km) **tri-oval** course doesn't look

much different from some other superspeedways. But any-

one who has driven the track knows how the Daytona Beach

breezes create their own problems and opportunities. Those

air flows make the 3,000-foot (915-meter) **backstretch**

at Daytona one of the fastest anywhere. That's why open-

wheel, Indy-style cars were quickly banned from the course.

The field at the 500 enters a turn packed tightly
together—at top speed!

They ran so fast, with so little weight, that they simply weren't safe.

The corners at Daytona can be even tougher than the backstretch. When Daytona opened in 1959, drivers felt as if their cars were being sucked forward as they tried to pass other cars on the turns, especially in the third turn. It wasn't long before drivers developed a signature maneuver, the "slingshot." This speedy move is nearly impossible for leaders to defend against.

Steeply banked turns (top) make Daytona a fast and challenging track.

Drivers use that extra "oomph" from the suction effect to zoom past a car ahead of them. Many Daytona 500 drivers have won with a slingshot move on a late lap.

Junior Johnson, one of the great early stock car racers, witnessed a similar Daytona oddity while winning the 500 in 1960. With nine laps to go, Junior was following leader Bobby Johns so closely that the suction blew out Johns's rear window and sent his Pontiac swerving. They call this suction effect the "draft."

Meanwhile, the turns at Daytona are tilted toward the center of the track at a jittery 31 degrees. How steep are these turns? If you're standing in the infield during a race, you can see the paint on the tops of the cars. The great Mario Andretti, who won the 500 in 1967, attacked these turns like no other driver. Most drivers back off and run wide against the outside retaining wall. Andretti gunned it down to the bottom of the track.

Wind and banking aren't the only elements drivers must

## THE DAYTONA 450?

The elements have affected the Daytona 500 on several occasions. Only the 1974 edition, however, took a hit from world economics. That race was shortened by 50 miles (83.4 km) due to the energy crisis forced by oil-producing countries. (It officially began on lap 21.) The drivers made up for lost time, however. They changed leads 60 times before Richard Petty finally crossed the finish line under the checkered flag.

Drivers in the Daytona 500 are in their seats racing full out for more than three hours.

deal with at Daytona. February can bring rain to Florida, and the raceway isn't spared. Three times the Daytona 500 has started under a **yellow caution flag** because of rain. Twice it was shortened because of rainfall. In 1965, the race was only 332.5 miles (555 km). A year later, it was shortened to 495 miles (831 km). In 1995, heavy rain **red-flagged** the race on lap 71, and drivers had to sit through a 1-hour 44-minute delay.

At least rain is better than snow. In 1977, winds from the northwest ripped through the back of the open grand-stands. Thousands of food wrappers and napkins swirled onto the track. Spectators said it looked like a blizzard. It would have been funny, except that some of the wrappers wound up on the **grilles** of cars. Stars such as Richard Petty, David Pearson, and Bobby Allison were done in by overheated engines. The paper kept air from cooling the powerful engines. Turns out the only opponents racers face at Daytona aren't their fellow drivers.

CHAPTER THREE

# The King and the Intimidator

Because the Daytona 500 is NASCAR's biggest event, it has welcomed every great stock car driver of the last 40 years. Twenty-six different drivers have taken home the trophy after the race. Two of them stand out from

When Petty retired in 1992, drivers and fans thanked him for his outstanding career.

the others, but for very different reasons.

They called Richard Petty "the King," and it isn't hard to figure out why. He won 200 Grand National/Winston Cup races in his career, almost double his nearest competitor. He won seven season championships, tied for the most. He also dominated NASCAR's biggest race, winning the Daytona 500 seven times.

Richard's father, Lee Petty, won the first Daytona 500 in 1959. Richard entered that race, too, finishing a lowly 57th out of 59 entries. It wouldn't be

Richard Petty took the checkered flag at Daytona seven times, including 1971 (top) and 1974.

long, however, before the son became racing's most popular figure. Part of the reason was Richard's big smile and down-to-earth manner. He rarely turned down an autograph request, especially from a kid. He was admired for his skillful driving.

In 1973, Petty won the 500 by more than two laps, an impressive feat. More often than that, he pulled out close races. In 1974, the King got a helping of luck. He and Donnie Allison each blew a tire while leading late in the race. Petty's went flat on the fourth turn, just before the pit area. Allison's went flat after the pit road. Petty got his changed quickly and won the race.

Dale Earnhardt, the other driver to win seven Winston Cup titles, had a very different Daytona experience. He won 33 races at other distances at the speedway, far more than any other racer. Oddly, he seemed unable to win the 500.

Earnhardt lost in the most surprising ways. In 1986, he was battling Geoff Bodine when he ran out of gas with three

laps to go. Earnhardt made it to the pit. To restart the engine, his crew sprayed **ether** in the **carburetor.** Unfortunately, this blew the engine. In 1990, he ran over a piece of metal with 1 mile (1.6 kilometers) to go and blew a tire. In 1995, he charged from fourteenth place to second in the final eight laps. At the end, however, he lost to Sterling Marlin by .61 of a second.

Finally, in 1998, the man they called "the Intimidator" brought home the Daytona 500 championship. As he drove down the **pit road** to Victory Lane, every crew lined up to congratulate him. Earnhardt then cruised into the infield

Dale Earnhardt's pit crew worked feverishly in 1995, but he lost by less than a second.

## GIVE AND TAKE

The fastest speed ever recorded in the Daytona 500 was 177.602 miles per hour (285.762 kilometers per hour), turned in by Buddy Baker in 1980. The fastest qualifying speed was a dizzying 210.364 miles per hour (338.476 kilometers per hour), by Bill Elliott in 1987.

Soon after that, NASCAR realized that speeds were becoming too high and unsafe. The circuit ordered all crews to install restrictor plates on their carburetors. These metal plates slowed the flow of air into the carburetor. This device in the engine mixes air and fuel to help create thousands of mini-explosions. These blasts power the pistons that make a car go. Thanks to the plates, less air meant less speed (but still a lot more speed than you'll get from your average family van!).

Bill Elliott (bottom left) steered his red No. 9 car to a record speed in 1987 and also won the 500.

grass. Whipping his car back and forth, his tires had carved

out a "3" in wide muddy strips. That, of course, was the

number of his car.

Earnhardt and Daytona are now linked forever. Three

years after that victory, the Intimidator died after crashing

on the final turn of the final lap of the 500. Daytona has

had many wonderful days. Earnhardt's death was one of

the sad days.

After finally winning in 1998, Earnhardt got high fives
from all the pit crews.

C H A P T E R   F O U R

# Races to Remember

Every edition of the Daytona 500 brings its own action and surprises. But some of the races have been extra special. Here are a few of them:

**1959** Considering the exciting ending of the first Daytona 500, it's no wonder they decided to make it an annual event. Lee Petty and Johnny Beauchamp roared down the homestretch, neck and neck. Little Joe Weatherly, who had been **lapped,** was there, too. The three cars sped across the finish line together. Nobody knew for sure who had won. Beauchamp was first declared the winner. However, after looking at photos and newsreel footage for three days, Big Bill France gave the victory to Petty.

Lee Petty (42) and Johnny Beauchamp dueled to the end in 1959, with Petty winning the first 500.

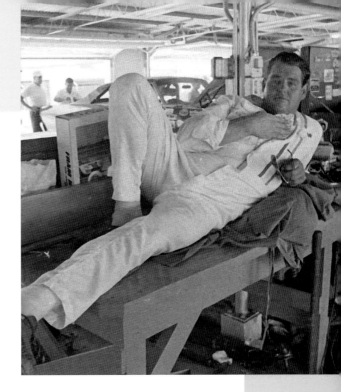

**1963** Anytime you meet a guy named "Tiny," chances are he's a giant. DeWayne (Tiny) Lund was no exception. He stood 6 feet 6 inches (198 centimeters) and weighed close to 300 pounds (136 kilograms). Lund was a good driver, but he arrived at the 1963 Daytona 500 with no car. Only when another driver, Marvin Panch, was injured did Lund get his chance. The owners of Panch's car, Glen and Leonard Wood, asked Tiny to fill in. He did, then ran off with the win.

**1968** Cale Yarborough and LeeRoy Yarbrough were two of the best racers of their era. They were not related. In fact, look closely and you'll notice they didn't spell their last names quite the same. Their names sure did sound alike. You can imagine how confused the TV audience was when Yarborough and Yarbrough dueled one another in 1968. Between the two of them, they led for 138 laps, trading back and forth. Cale finally

Big "Tiny" Lund took up a lot of room. In 1963, they made room for him on the victory stand.

took the lead for good with a slingshot move on lap 197.

**1988** Bobby Allison had already won the Daytona 500 twice, but this one was different. Bobby took the lead with 17 laps to go. He had only one young racer to fight off—his son, Davey Allison. Bobby hit the gas and took the checkered flag by two car lengths. Davey, who would win the Daytona 500 in 1992, called it the happiest day in his life.

**1989** Darrell Waltrip had been in 16 Daytona 500s without winning a single one of them. In 1989, it looked like Dale Earnhardt and Ken Schrader had the two fastest cars. They both had to pit for gas with 11 laps to go. Meanwhile, Waltrip stayed on the track and hoped he wouldn't run dry, too. A couple of times he had to jerk his wheel on the turns, shaking drops of fuel into the engine. Amazingly, he made it across the finish line first

Bobby Allison won his third Daytona 500 by holding off his son, Davey, at the end.

before finally running out of fuel.

**1999** By the end of the twentieth century, Jeff Gordon was the NASCAR driver to beat. He had won the 1997 race at the tender age of 25. He had millions of fans, but a lot of drivers resented the young man's fast success. After Gordon won the pole in 1999, no one was going to let him take the race without a fight. He got bumped and boxed all day. Toward the end, teammates Dale Earnhardt and Mike Skinner twice tried to push one another past Gordon. Both times, Gordon put himself in line to "steal" the push. He earned his second Daytona 500 win.

The Daytona 500 is always a special race, a highlight of every racing season. Every February, it's the place to go to see the very best stock car racers go for the highest honor in the sport.

Jeff Gordon (bottom right) leads the field from the pole at the 1999 Daytona 500.

## THREE KINGS

Jeff Gordon won the 1997 Daytona 500, but the hero of the day was Rick Hendrick.
He owned Gordon's car. He owned the second- and third-place finishers as well.
Gordon, Terry Labonte, and Ricky Craven became the first teammates ever to finish
one-two-three in a Winston Cup event.

Five hundred miles (805 kilometers) later, Gordon was
still in front, holding off a hard-charging Dale Earnhardt
to win.

# A HISTORY OF THE DAYTONA 500

**1903**   The first race between horseless carriages, or autos, occurs on the beach at Daytona, Florida.

**1936**   Stock car racing begins at Daytona Beach.

**1947**   William H. G. (Big Bill) France founds NASCAR.

**1957**   Ground is cleared for Daytona International Speedway.

**1959**   Lee Petty wins the first Daytona 500, edging Johnny Beauchamp in a photo finish.

**1974**   The Daytona 500 officially begins on lap 21, shortened 50 miles because of a national energy crisis.

**1980**   Buddy Baker sets a Daytona 500 record with an average speed of 177.602 miles per hour  (285.762 kilometers per hour).

**1987**   NASCAR orders all Daytona crews to put restrictor plates on their carburetors, reducing air flow, power, and speed.

**1995**   The Daytona 500 is delayed 1 hour and 44 minutes because of rain.

**1996**   Daytona USA, a multimillion-dollar motorsports attraction and theme park, opens to the public at Daytona International Speedway.

**1997**   At 25 years, 6 months, Jeff Gordon becomes the youngest driver to win the Daytona 500.

**1998**   Dale Earnhardt finally wins the Daytona 500 on his twentieth try.

# GLOSSARY

**backstretch**—the long straightaway that is on the opposite side of a race track from the start/finish line

**banked**—tilted toward the inside edge

**carburetor**—an engine part that helps make small explosions by mixing fuel and air; these explosions power the pistons that make the car move

**checkered flag**—a black-and-white checked flag waved at the winner as he crosses the finish line at the end of a race

**ether**—a flammable liquid made from ethyl alcohol and sulfuric acid

**grilles**—metal gratings at the front of a car that protect the mechanical parts while allowing air to flow through

**infield**—the area within the racecourse

**lapped**—when a racer has been passed by another car that is a full lap ahead

**pit road**—the area where mechanical crews work on cars at a race

**photo finish**—a race result that is so close that photographs must be used to determine who crossed the finish line first

**purse**—the total amount of money offered at a race or other event

**red-flagged**—a signal that a race has been suspended because of dangerous conditions; drivers must leave the track immediately

**tri-oval**—a track design that adds an extra mild curve along the backstretch to the traditional oval shape

**yellow caution flag**—a signal that all drivers must slow to the same speed while the track is made safe for racing

# FOR MORE INFORMATION ABOUT THE DAYTONA 500

## Books

Center, Bill. *Ultimate Stock Car*. New York: DK Publishing, 2000.

Ethan, Eric. *Daytona 500*. Milwaukee: Gareth Stephens, 1999.

Libby, Bill with Richard Petty. *King Richard:The Richard Petty Story*. New York: Doubleday, 1977.

## Web Sites

### Daytona International Speedway
*http://www.DaytonaInternationalSpeedway.com*
The official site of the home of the Daytona 500 includes a map of the track, directions to Daytona, and information on purchasing tickets for races.

### Daytona 500
*http://www.Daytona500.com*
The official site of the race itself contains complete race results, previews of upcoming races, features on history, and more.

# INDEX

## ABOUT THE AUTHOR

Phil Barber spent eight years as an editor for NFL Publishing. He now writes for *NFL Insider*, NFL.com, and other league projects. He has also covered football, basketball, and baseball for *The Sporting News*. Barber's book credits include *The NFL Experience* and *Superstars of the NFL*. He co-wrote *Football America*, *The NFL Century*, and *NFL's Greatest*. He lives about a mile from Calistoga Speedway in California, with his wife Kara Brunzell and a multitude of daughters (four, actually, but it sometimes seems like more).